Adventures

Race to the Pyramid

Karen Ball • Jonatronix

Max's mission log

We are travelling through space on board the micro-ship Excelsa with our new friends, Nok and Seven.

We're on a mission to save Planet Exis (Nok's home planet), which is running out of power. We need to collect four fragments that have been hidden throughout the Beta-Prime Galaxy. Together the fragments form the Core of Exis. Only the Core will restore power to the planet.

It's not easy. A space villain called Badlaw wants the power of the Core for himself. His army of robotic Krools is never far behind us!

Fragments collected so far: 1

Current location: Planet Celeston

In our last adventure …

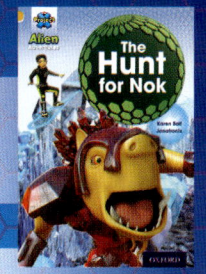

Cat and I went to rescue Nok, who had been captured by some Minatrolls. We rescued a pyrite panther instead and followed it to a huge pyramid. We think Nok and the fragment are inside.

We had to cross a moat of bubbling liquid to get to the pyramid. Then the Krools arrived!

The pyrite panther opened a secret entrance and we followed it into the pyramid.

Chapter 1 – Signal search

Ant, Tiger and Seven stared at the communi-screen.

"Max?" said Ant. "Can you hear me?"

There was a hiss and a crackle and then nothing.

"How are we going to find them?" asked Tiger.

Seven thought for a moment. "I'll see if I can pick up a signal from Max's watch." He tapped at the control panel and a map appeared. He pointed to a flashing area on the map. "They're at the Crystal Pyramid of Celeston."

"What are we waiting for?" said Tiger. "Let's go!"

The Crystal Pyramid of Celeston

Information

The Crystal Pyramid of Celeston was built by the Minatrolls. At the heart of the pyramid is a large chamber. Inside it are the Minatrolls' treasures. They keep them in ruby cages.

Tunnels
- More than 50 tunnels lead to the treasure chamber.

Valuable treasures
- Fragment of Exis
- Cup of Stromalin
- Armour of Nemor

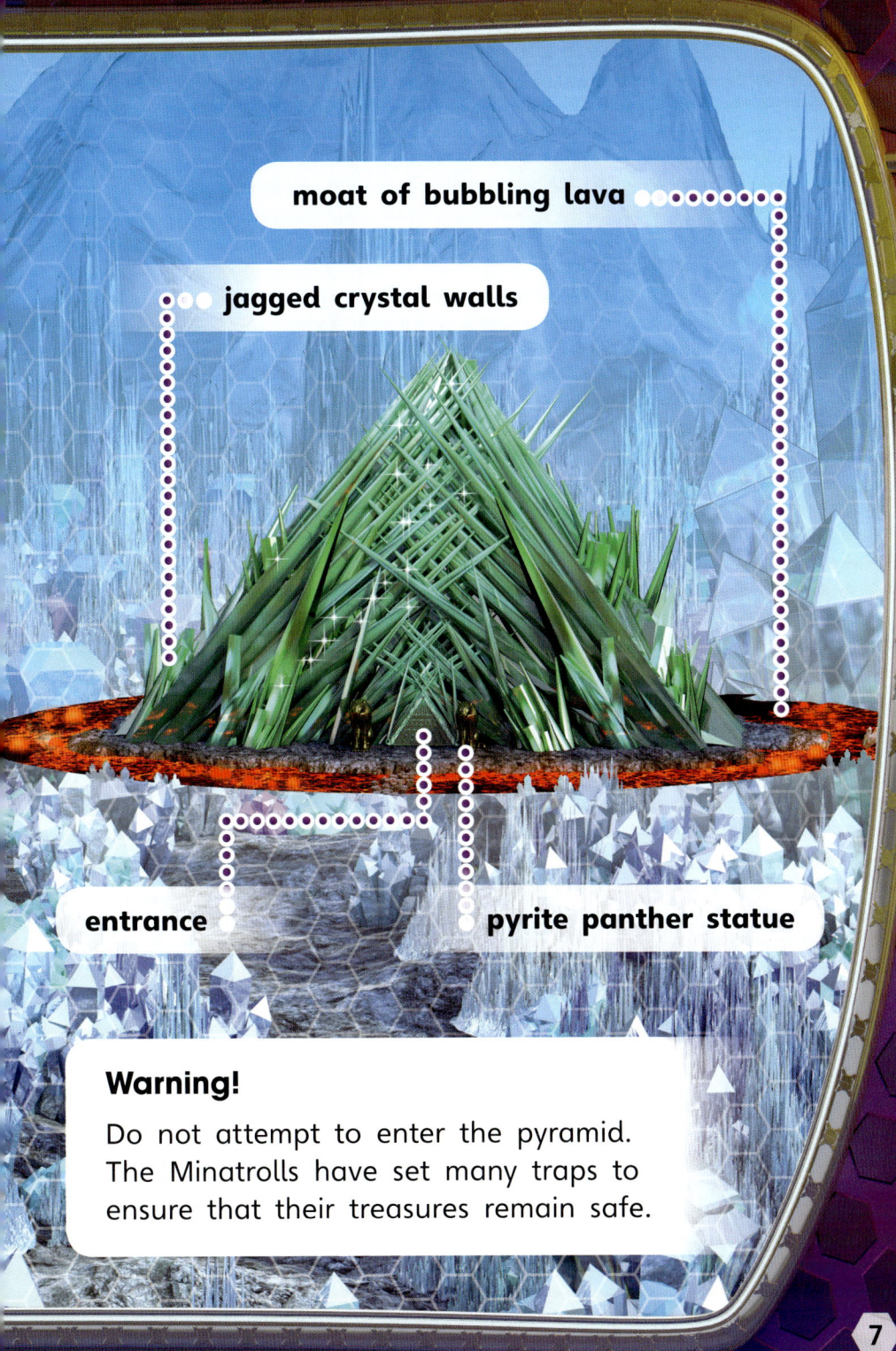

Warning!

Do not attempt to enter the pyramid. The Minatrolls have set many traps to ensure that their treasures remain safe.

Tiger glanced over at the pilot's chair. "Right, how do we fly this thing?" he said. Nok was normally the one at the controls.

"I think I know how to fly it," said Ant. "Nok did give me a flying lesson ... once."

Chapter 2 – Learning to fly

Ant pulled the steering orbs back. The ship wobbled in the air.

"I think I'm getting the hang of this," he said.

Suddenly the ship began to roll over and over.

"I feel sick," said Tiger.

"Sorry!" said Ant.

Up ahead, they could see a dark smudge in the sky.

"It looks like a storm," said Ant.

Soon, they were struggling to see anything through the thick clouds.

"We should land and wait for the storm to pass," said Seven.

"We need to keep going. The others might be in danger," said Tiger. "We must be nearly at the pyramid by now!"

Ant pushed the steering orbs again. The ship jerked forwards. Outside, the heavy rain crashed down.

Then, all of a sudden, the ship flew clear of the clouds … and Ant gulped. They were flying straight towards a cliff face.

"Pull up!" yelled Seven.

Ant pulled back hard on the steering orbs. The ship shot up, just missing the solid wall of rock.

As they flew over the cliff, a huge pyramid loomed in front of them.

Ant steered the ship towards it. The ship began to judder.

"Prepare yourselves for a rough landing!" Ant called.

Chapter 3 – A way in

As they approached the pyramid, they looked out at the ground below.

"There are Krools everywhere!" gasped Tiger. He pointed to the army of green robots.

"I can't risk setting the ship down here," said Ant.

"I'll teleport down and try to find a way inside the pyramid," said Tiger. "You find somewhere safe to land."

"OK," said Ant. "Be careful."

Tiger left the bridge and quickly made his way to the teleport chamber.

A moment later, Tiger found himself standing by the entrance to the pyramid. He looked over at the Krools on the other side of the moat. "I think I'll stay micro-size!" he said to himself.

The Krools didn't notice Tiger. They were too busy trying to get across the moat.

Tiger saw one Krool sink into the bubbling liquid. "They're bound to get across soon," he thought. "I'd better find a way in, quickly."

Tiger pushed the door of the pyramid, but it wouldn't budge. Tiger knew he could not open it while he was micro-size. He also knew the Krools would spot him if he grew. Just then, Ant appeared by his side.

"I've left Seven to look after the ship," Ant told him.

Tiger glanced over his shoulder. He saw that a Krool had made it halfway across the stones. The other Krools weren't far behind.

"We have to get inside now!" said Tiger. Ant began to examine the door.

Chapter 4 – The hidden enemy

"This is hopeless," Tiger said. "We're never going to get inside."

He slumped back against one of the statues next to the door and sat down.

Something clicked. The door slid open.

"You did it!" cried Ant. "There must have been a hidden switch on that statue."

They ran inside and the door slammed shut behind them.

Away from the watchful eyes of the Krools, Ant and Tiger grew back to normal size.

The air inside the pyramid was dry and still.

"Max? Cat?" Ant called. His voice echoed around the chamber. There was no reply.

They took a few steps further into the pyramid.

"What do we do now?" asked Tiger.

Ahead of them were three passages. Ant pointed to one of them. "I think we should go that …"

Before Ant could finish what he was saying, a cold metallic voice stopped him.

"Surrender, Earth creatures." Out of the shadows, Krool 1, commander of Badlaw's army, stepped forward.

They hadn't escaped the Krools, after all.

Find out what happens next in *One Step Ahead*.